Hi there!
I'm Bertie Bacteriun

Let's meet my friends...

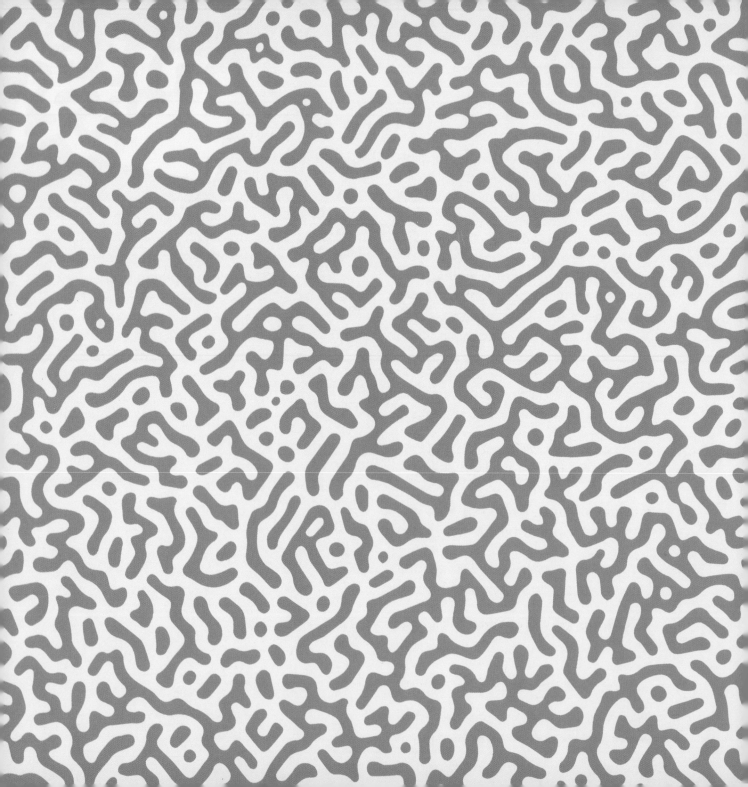

Meet The Germs

This book is dedicated by 'Grumpy Gramps'
to grandsons Matthew, Cameron and Magnus.

The boys provided the inspiration for an old
microbiologist to produce a children's book and
gave Matthew the opportunity to develop
his drawing talents.

Meet The Germs

Written by Alan Bruce
Illustrated by Matthew Bruce and Alan Bruce

Bertie Bacterium

I'm Bertie the bacterium,
a friendly wee germ,
I live on your skin but don't cause any harm.
I'm fat and round but oh so small,
you can look, but I am sure
you won't find me at all.

A million of me you could fit on a pin,
so looking for me - where do you begin?
Finding me, you haven't a hope,
unless you use a microscope.

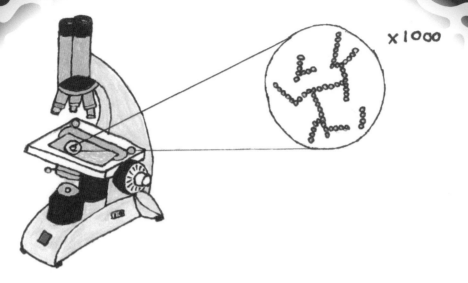

x1000

Not all my pals are as friendly as me,
when you meet them, I'm sure you'll agree.
There's Pete and Amy, Freddie and Molly,
though Vicky and Sid are not quite so jolly.

That leaves Yeasty, who's a bit of a lad,
sometimes he's good but sometimes he's bad.
We're known as the Germs so let's meet the team,
we may cause a surprise but we won't
make you scream.

Molly Mushroom

I'm Molly the mushroom
and live in the forest,
You're sure to find me
where it's wettest and warmest,
I grow in the soil or sometimes in wood,
and people can even eat me as food.

But you have to be careful,
some mushrooms are poisonous,
to eat the wrong one can be pretty dangerous.
A red and white toadstool is a beautiful thing,
but eat one and you'll soon be vomiting.

But stick with Molly and you won't go wrong,
with the rest of the gang is where I belong.
I'm a friendly little germ, always happy and jolly,
and if it comes on rain
I can act as a brolly.

Sid Salmonella

I'm Sid Salmonella, a nasty little fella,
I can cause a sore tummy
and make you cry for your mummy.
I am sometimes in milk
or in eggs that are rotten,
and a meeting with me
won't be quickly forgotten.

I am sometimes in cheese and often in meat,
but not if they're fresh and ready to eat.
I only like foods that are bitter and smelly,
so you'll never find me in sweets or in jelly.

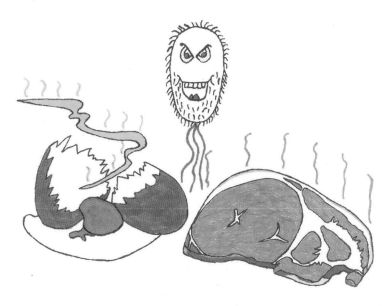

Of the other Germs I like Vicky the best,
as just like me she is often a pest.
Vicky and I can get up to no good,
be it causing disease or
spoiling your food.

Amy Amoeba

I'm Amy Amoeba and I look a bit weird,
but no need to worry, I am not to be feared.
I may just look like a big blob of gunk,
or even a jelly that has suddenly shrunk.

I have no arms or legs but
can alter my shape,
and if I'm in trouble I can quickly escape.
Though I cannot run to where I need to go,
like a droplet of water I just go with the flow.

I can be square or round, short or tall,
and the Germs call me, when they want to play ball,
I am the best goalie and my teammates don't fret,
because when I'm in goal nothing
gets in the net.

Vicky Virus

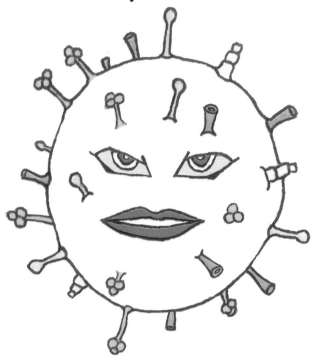

I'm Vicky, a virus and I live in your body,
if I infect you, you might need a hot toddy.
I'll give you the cold or even the flu,
make you cough or sneeze and say
'AAA...choo'.

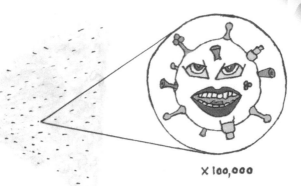

X 100,000

Sid and I, cause mayhem and harm,
and when we're together it's a cause for alarm.
We will make you feel ill, that is for sure,
but a trip to the doctor will soon find a cure.

The doctor may treat you for all of your ills,
and send you off home with some lotions or pills.
So Vicky and Sid will need to move quick,
or the doctor will prescribe an antibiotic.

Freddie Fungus

My name is Freddie and I'm pretty shy,
but to all my friends I'm just a fun guy!
Although I look both shaggy and hairy,
take it from me, I'm not at all scary.

I like any foods that are sugary sweet,
and growing on jam is a special treat.
I also like vegetables and freshly picked fruit,
so you'll find me on peaches or even beetroot.

When I grow on foods they
get covered in mould,
and in such a state they're
not fit to be sold.
I can grow in a fridge
on top of your cheese,
but don't breathe me in
or I'll make you sneeze.

Protozoa Pete

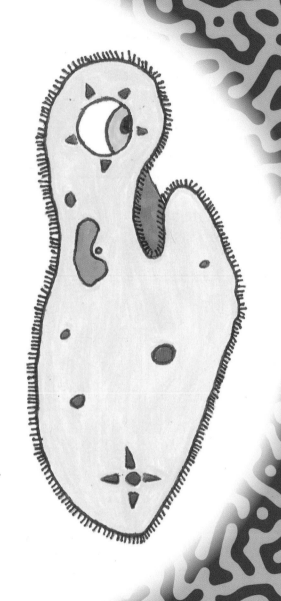

I am Protozoa Pete, and
don't smell so sweet,
I live in dirty water, and love
it when it's hotter.
A pond for me is the
perfect location,
better still with contamination.

I often love to guddle
in a nice mucky puddle,
where I can splash and swim to keep in trim.
If it's grimy or slimy or has a strong pong,
then that is the place where I belong.

The rest of the Germs think I am a bit whiffy,
But if they give me a call I'll be there in a jiffy.
And just to be certain I'm not left on my own,
I'll make sure that I spray on some
Eau de Cologne.

Yeasty Boy

I'm Yeasty Boy and you
should give me a call,
if you're ever in need
of some alcohol.
I can make beer or wine,
but gin is more risky,
but I'm an expert at making
good old Scotch whisky.

I can help you bake cakes
and all kinds of bread,
and I'm also to be found in Marmite spread.
I live on the surface of fresh grapes and plums,
but I never sit still and twiddle my thumbs.

I'm mischievous and playful and so full of pep,
that I sometimes end up on the naughty step.
I love to play pranks on the rest of the Germs,
but we always end up on the best of terms.

So that's Bertie and Sid, Vicky and Pete,
Molly and Amy and we're almost complete,
Together with Freddie we have fun and enjoy,
all the pranks played by Yeasty Boy.

You've now had the chance to meet the full squad,
I hope you don't think that we're creepy or odd.
We live all around you and exist on your terms,
but are really just a bunch of friendly old Germs!!

The Germs

Bertie

SID

VICKY

PETE

Molly

Amy

Freddie

Yeasty Boy

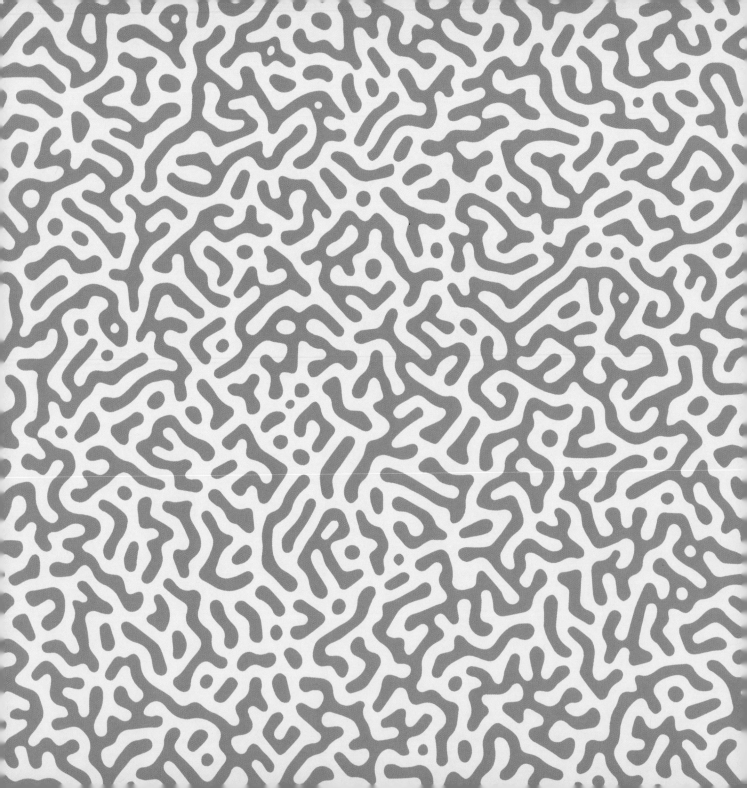

Printed in Great Britain
by Amazon

37086035R00016